9-03

12/11 0X Marked missing

GEOGRAPHY OF THE WORLD

EUROPE

By Cynthia Klingel

THE CHILD'S WORLD®
CHANHASSEN, MINNESOTA

Published in the United States of America by The Child's World®
P.O. Box 326, Chanhassen, MN 55317-0326
800-599-READ
www.childsworld.com

Photo Credits: Cover: O, Alamany & E. Vicens/Corbis; Animals Animals/Earth
Scenes: 7 (Henry Ausloos), 18 (Robert Maier); Archivo Iconografico, S.A./Corbis: 21,
22; Corbis: 6 (Michael Busselle), 9 (Yann Arthus-Bertrand), 11 (Ralph A. Clevenger),
17 (Staffan Widstrand), 17 (Francesc Muntada), 27 (Chris Rainer); Dean
Conger/Corbis: 9, 24; Picture Desk: 14 (Travelsite/Jarrold Publishing), 16
(Travelsite/Colosanti), Travelsite/Neil Setchfield/Picture Desk: 20, 23.

The Child's World®: Mary Berendes, Publishing Director
Editorial Directions, Inc.: E. Russell Primm, Editorial Director; Pam Rosenberg, Line
Editor; Katie Marsico, Assistant Editor; Olivia Nellums, Editorial Assistant; Susan
Hindman, Copy Editor; Elizabeth K. Martin, Proofreader; Ann Grau Duvall, Peter
Garnham, Carol Yehling, Fact Checkers; Dr. Charles Maynara, Professor of Geography,
Radford University, Radford, Virginia, Subject Consultant; Tim Griffin/IndexServ,
Indexer; Cian Loughlin O'Day, Photo Researcher; Elizabeth K. Martin, Photo Selector;
XNR Productions, Inc., Cartographer

Library of Congress Cataloging-in-Publication Data
Klingel, Cynthia Fitterer.
  Europe / by Cynthia Klingel.
    p. cm. — (Geography of the world series)
Includes index.
Summary: Introduces the geography, topography, and climate of the continent
of Europe.
  ISBN 1-59296-060-X (lib. bdg. : alk. paper)
  1. Europe—Geography—Juvenile literature. 2. Natural history—Europe—Juvenile
literature. [1. Europe—Geography.] I. Title. II. Series.
  D1051.K58 2003
  914—dc21   2003006342

TABLE OF CONTENTS

CHAPTER ONE

WHERE IS EUROPE?

Europe is located in the Northern **Hemisphere.** It is connected to the western edge of Asia and shares two countries—Russia and Turkey—with that continent. Europe stretches from 25° west **longitude** to 60° east longitude and from 71° north **latitude** to 35° north latitude. Europe is located to the north of Africa. Its northernmost tip falls north of the Arctic Circle. Because of its shape, Europe has many **peninsulas.** No place in Europe is very far from an ocean or a sea. It is also the only continent that does not have a desert.

UNIQUE CONTINENTS

Each continent is somewhat different from the others, with its own unique history. The weather, landscape, and plant and animal life of each continent depend on several different factors. These influences include where a continent sits on the planet, how close to or far from the equator it is located, and the amount and types of bodies of water that are found there.

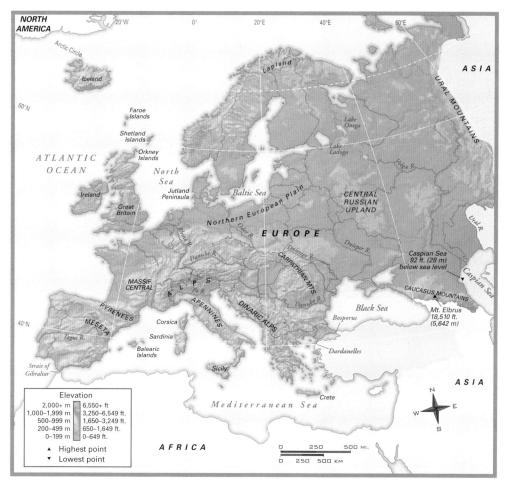

A physical map of Europe

There are four main land areas in Europe: the Central **Plain,** the

Central Uplands, the Alpine Mountain System, and the Northwestern

Uplands. The Central Plain is a mostly flat, V-shaped area that begins

at the Atlantic Ocean on the western coast of France. It reaches to the

eastern border of Europe and ends in a wide band that stretches from the Arctic Ocean to the Black Sea. Europe's largest cities are in the Central Plain region.

The Central Uplands stretch from the western coast of Spain to Poland. They lie between the Central Plains and the Alpine Mountain System. This is an area of forests

The Black Forest in Germany is the setting for many famous tales, such as Little Red Riding Hood and Snow White.

and **plateaus** such as the

Meseta, the Massif

Central, the Ardennes,

the Black Forest, and the

Bohemian Forest.

The Pyrenees Mountains separating Spain and France are more than 350 miles (563 kilometers) long.

The Alpine Mountain System runs through southern Europe from Spain to the southern part of western Russia. This mountain chain includes the Sierra Nevada, the Pyrenees, the Alps, and the Apennines.

The Northwestern Uplands are high plateaus, rugged mountains, and deep valleys that can be found in northern France, the United Kingdom, Norway, and Sweden. The soil here is usually very rocky and not good for farming.

CHAPTER TWO

HOW DID EUROPE COME TO BE?

Europe is one of seven continents on Earth. It covers about 4,000,000 square miles (10,360,000 square kilometers) and is the sixth largest continent. Australia is the only continent smaller than Europe. Europe sits on a large peninsula of the great Eurasian landmass.

Much of Europe is surrounded by water. To the north is the Arctic Ocean, and to the west is the Atlantic Ocean. The Baltic Sea and the North Sea connect to the Atlantic and border some of the northern coasts. Waters to the south include the Mediterranean Sea, the Strait of Gibraltar, the Black Sea, and the Sea

RIVERS

The three longest rivers in Europe are the Volga, the Danube, and the Rhine. The Volga, in Russia, is almost 2,200 miles (3,530 km) long. The Danube flows through the center of Europe for about 1,770 miles (2,850 km). The Rhine, in west-central Europe, flows for 820 miles (1,320 km).

of Marmara. The Caspian Sea forms part of the southeast boundary.

Some of Europe's boundaries are shaped by landforms and waterways. The Ural Mountains and the Ural River form the eastern boundary with Asia. The Caucasus Mountains are part of the southeastern border, and two straits, the Bosporus and the Dardanelles, form portions of the southern border.

The Strait of Gibraltar is the gateway to the Mediterranean Sea that separates Europe from Africa. Though the Caucasus Mountains, above right, are mainly in Asia, the range's largest mountain, Mount Elbrus is in the European part of Russia.

Europe was not formed all at once, like many of the other continents. The formation of Europe began more than 3 billion years ago. It is believed that pieces of Europe from different periods in the formation of Earth came together at different times to result in one continent.

For example, some regions in the European countries of Finland, Norway, Scotland, Russia, and Bulgaria are made from the oldest known rock on Earth. Other rocks provide evidence that, at a later time, pieces of Africa broke off and became connected with these older formations. The countries of Great Britain and Ireland have a **geological** history that is completely different from other areas of Europe.

Cliffs off the western coast of Ireland show the many layers of rock formed over time.

The southern part of Europe, especially Italy, is home to

volcanoes and earthquakes. The Earth is constantly changing and

shifting, and some of this activity occurs under southern Europe.

Other events are occurring today that continue to change the geog-

raphy of Europe. For example, the Alps, a large European mountain

range, grow taller each year because of activity happening deep

within the Earth.

CHAPTER THREE

WHAT MAKES EUROPE SPECIAL?

Europe is not a large continent. It is not home to the tallest mountain in the world or to the highest waterfall. But visitors to the continent will be treated to many spectacular sights.

In Norway, visitors can see fabulous fjords. Fjords are huge valleys created by **glaciers.** After the glaciers left, water filled the bottoms of the valleys. Mountains rise up on either side, topped by snow-capped peaks. Many people travel to Norway to take boat trips into the fjords.

The Caspian Sea is really a saltwater lake. It is the largest lake in the world and covers 143,250 square miles (371,000 sq km). It is located in the southeastern corner of Europe. The Caspian Sea lies in both Europe and Asia.

A political map of Europe

The Alpine Mountain System has several beautiful ranges. Many people travel to the Swiss Alps every year to vacation. The highest mountain in Europe is Mount Elbrus, in the Caucasus Mountains. It is 18,510 feet (5,642 meters) above sea level.

Giant's Causeway is a strange rock formation on the coast of Ireland.

Ireland is home to a strange rock formation called Giant's

Causeway. It is an area filled with stone columns or pillars. The

columns are usually about 12 inches (30 centimeters) across. Some are

as high as 40 feet (12 m). Giant's Causeway looks like a huge stairway

for giants climbing from the ocean onto the shore. It was formed long

ago from lava—liquid rock—pushed up through the Earth's surface,

cooling, and then cracking.

Visitors to Europe can also sample many different **cultures.**

The continent is home to 47 countries, each special in its own way.

And because Europe is one of the smallest continents, it is easy for

visitors to explore several countries in one trip.

Countries in northern Europe have longer, colder winters than

the rest of Europe. But, in general, the **climate** of Europe changes

very little from the north to the south. It has a temperate climate. This

means that temperatures there don't

usually get extremely hot or extremely

cold. This is partly due to the effect of

warm waters from the Gulf of Mexico.

The Atlantic Ocean's Gulf Stream

brings these waters north to an area

off the coast of Newfoundland. From

**LAND OF THE
MIDNIGHT SUN**

There are countries in
the northernmost part of
Europe where the sun is
out almost all night long
during the summer. This is
the result of how Earth is
tilted. But it also means
that during the winter, it is
dark almost all day and
night in these countries.

The Geiranger Fjord in Norway is just one of the many fjords or inlets formed by the receding glaciers at the end of the Ice Age.

there, the North Atlantic Drift carries the warmer waters to western Europe and Scandinavia. When air passes over the North Atlantic Drift, it gets warmer. This warmer air helps keep the temperatures on land mild.

CHAPTER FOUR

WHAT ANIMALS AND PLANTS ARE FOUND IN EUROPE?

Many kinds of plants and animals live in Europe. Europe's **habitats** include forests, grasslands, tundra, and high mountains. **Coniferous** forests are found mostly in northern Europe.

A female brown bear leads her cubs into a clearing in a Finnish forest. Top right, conifer forests cover the slopes of this Catalonian valley in Spain.

Reindeer living in northern European countries such as Norway are similar to North America's caribou.

WHITE STORKS

Many Europeans consider it good luck to have a pair of white storks build a nest in their chimney. White storks are very large migrating birds. They mate for life and return to the same place every year to build a nest. They nest in chimneys, on roofs, and in church towers.

The trees in these forests are called

conifers. Some of the more common

conifers in Europe are the fir, pine, spruce,

and larch. There are **deciduous** forests

in central and southern Europe. These forests are home to elm, oak,

maple, ash, and birch. In the south, broadleaf evergreens like the cork and the olive can be found. Grasslands, in Ukraine and south-eastern Russia, are home to a variety of grasses. The tundra and high mountains are not easy places for plants to grow. Mosses, flowers, lichens, and small shrubs can be found there.

Common **mammals** living in Europe include foxes, wolves, reindeer, elk, deer, hedgehogs, rabbits, wild boars, moles, and European brown bears. Birds such as eagles, falcons, owls, ravens, and finches are native to Europe. Many types of fish can be found in the waters off the long coastline of Europe. Herring, salmon, sturgeon, trout, tuna, mackerel, sardine, cod, and flounder are fished from these waters.

Most of the animals in Europe are

REINDEER

Many people are fascinated by the wild reindeer native to northern Europe. The North American version of reindeer is the caribou found in Alaska. People of the northern part of Scandinavia are called Saami. They herd the reindeer, most of which are no longer wild.

Fishing boats in a port on the Greek island of Crete.

rarely seen in the wild. Over the years, their natural habitats have been

destroyed by people. The animals now live in areas that are difficult

for humans to find or get to. Some native animals are protected in

national parks and in zoos.

CHAPTER FIVE

WHO LIVES IN EUROPE?

There are approximately 727 million people living in Europe today.

People have lived in Europe for many hundreds of thousands of

years. But it wasn't until about 6,000 years ago that these early people

formed villages. Before that, many tribes of people traveled from place

to place. As they traveled, they mixed with people of other tribes. Some

The rise of farming in the Middle Ages helped organize people into villages.

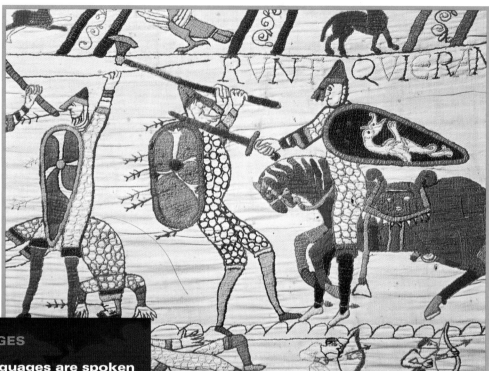

The cultures of many countries of Europe have been changed over the years by wars and invasions. The famous Bayeux Tapestry (above) tells of the French invasion of England in 1066.

of the earliest villages in Europe were on the islands east of Greece.

In the last 2,000 years, different groups of people have moved in and out of Europe. Wars between the groups were fought to gain control of the land. Each group brought its own culture to the region.

*Polish dancers perform a traditional Polish dance
in Warsaw's Old Town Square*

RELIGIONS

The most common religion in Europe is Christianity. Many Christians in Europe belong to the Roman Catholic faith. Other Christian groups in Europe include Protestants and members of the Greek Orthodox church.

Today, many different **ethnic groups** can still be found in Europe. Some countries are home to people from two or more ethnic groups. Europe also has many people who have moved there from non-European countries. They have brought their native cultures with them. More and more Europeans are of African or Asian descent.

CHAPTER SIX

WHAT IS EUROPE
LIKE TODAY?

Today, Europe is densely populated. Only Asia—the largest continent—is home to more people. The European country of the Netherlands is one of the world's most densely populated countries.

The largest cities in Europe are London, Moscow, St. Petersburg,

St. Basil's Cathedral stands in the background of this busy intersection in Moscow's Red Square.

and Paris. Over time, many Europeans have left small towns and villages and moved to cities.

The cities of Western Europe are successful and well developed. The cities in Eastern Europe have struggled to be successful. Business and industry are not as well developed there, so people living there do not enjoy the same opportunities as those in the western cities. The leaders of Eastern Europe are working hard to bring more industries to their cities.

Most people living in Europe are well educated. More than nine out of ten Europeans can read and write. In some parts of Europe, though, life is not as easy. Fewer people can read and write in the countries of Albania, Malta, Portugal, and the part of Turkey that falls

EUROPEAN UNION

Many European countries belong to an organization called the European Union (EU). It was formed in 1992 with the Maastricht Treaty. The EU provides ways for its member countries to work together. The policies formed by the EU first took effect in 1993.

in Europe. The governments in some countries are not stable. For instance, Bosnia and Herzegovina has recently suffered through a war. Many of its people are homeless, hungry, and out of work. Leaders in Europe and around the world continue to look for solutions to these problems.

In the past 15 years, many countries in Eastern Europe have experienced changes in government. In fact, some areas that were republics under the Soviet Union and Yugoslavia became countries with their own governments. These are Estonia, Latvia, Lithuania, Belarus, Moldova, Ukraine, Croatia, Macedonia, Slovenia, and Bosnia and Herzegovina. In 1993, the former country of Czechoslovakia split into the Czech Republic and Slovakia.

RUSSIA

Russia is the largest country in the world. It covers 6,592,800 square miles (17,075,400 sq km). The majority of Russia's people live on the continent of Europe. But it is not just a European country. Part of Russia is also on the continent of Asia.

A Bosnian woman walks past the ruins of a bombed building in Sarajevo, the capital of Bosnia-Herzegovina.

In the past few years, some countries in the European Union have agreed to use the same type of money. This new currency is called the Euro. The use of the Euro should make it easier for Europeans and people visiting Europe to travel and do business in countries other than their own.

The countries of Europe have a rich geographic and cultural history. Their peoples and their leaders continue to use the lessons learned from the past to make decisions for the future.

Glossary

climate (KLYE-mit) A climate is the kind of weather that usually occurs in a place.

coniferous (kuh-NIF-ur-uhss) A coniferous forest is one that is made up of trees that bear cones and have needle-like leaves.

culture (KUHL-chur) A culture is the way of life, customs, and traditions of a group of people.

deciduous (di-SIJ-oo-uhss) A deciduous forest is made up mainly of trees that shed their leaves each year.

dialects (DYE-uh-lekts) A dialect is the way a language is spoken by a particular group of people in a particular place.

ethnic groups (ETH-nik groops) An ethnic group is made up of people who share a common country of origin, language, and culture.

geological (jee-uh-LAH-ji-kuhl) Something that is geological has to do with the study of the history of Earth through the examination of its rocks and soil.

glaciers (GLAY-shurs) Glaciers are huge sheets of ice.

habitats (HAB-uh-tats) Habitats are the environments in which plants and animals live.

hemisphere (HEM-uhss-fihr) One half of a sphere, such as the northern half or southern half of Earth when it is divided in two by the equator, is called a hemisphere.

latitude (LAT-uh-tood) Latitude is the position of a place on the globe as it is measured in degrees north or south of the equator.

longitude (LON-juh-tood) Longitude is the position of a place on the globe as it is measured in degrees east or west of an imaginary line known as the prime meridian. The prime meridian runs through the Greenwich Observatory in London, England, and is sometimes called the Greenwich Meridian.

mammals (MAM-uhls) Mammals are warm-blooded animals with backbones. One important characteristic of mammals is that females produce milk to feed their young.

peninsula (puh-NIN-suh-luh) A peninsula is a piece of land that sticks out from a larger piece of land and is almost completely surrounded by water.

plain (PLANE) A plain is a large area of land that is flat.

plateau (plah-TOH) A plateau is a raised, flat area of land.

A European Almanac

Location on the Globe:
Longitude: 25° west to 60° east
Latitude: 71° north to 35° north

Greatest distance from north to south: 3,000 miles (4,800 km)

Greatest distance from east to west: 4,000 miles (6,400 km)

Borders: Arctic Ocean, Atlantic Ocean, Mediterranean Sea, Black Sea, Kuma-Manych Depression, Caspian Sea, Ural Mountains, Zhem River

Total Area: 4,038,000 square miles (10,458,000 sq km)

Highest Point: Mount Elbrus, 18,510 feet (5,642 m) above sea level

Lowest Point: Caspian Sea shore, 92 feet (28 m) below sea level

Number of Countries on the Continent: 47

Major Mountain Ranges: Alps, Appenines, Balkans, Carpathians, Caucusus, Pyrenees, Sierra Nevada

Major Deserts: None

Major Rivers: Danube, Don, Elbe, Rhine, Rhone, Seine, Volga

Major Lakes: Caspian Sea, Ladoga

Major Cities:
Moscow, Russia
London, United Kingdom
Paris, France
Rome, Italy
Athens, Greece
St. Petersburg, Russia

Languages: About 50 languages are spoken in Europe. Some of these include Bulgarian, Czech, Polish, Russian, Danish, English, German, Swedish, French, Italian, and Spanish.

Population: 703,400,000 (estimated 2000)

Religions: Christianity, Judaism, Islam

Mineral Resources: Natural gas, coal, petroleum, iron ore, chromite, lead manganese, nickel, platinum, potash, silver, zinc

Europe in the News

130,000 B.C.–35,000 B.C.	Neanderthals inhabit the continent of Europe.
40,000 B.C.–10,000 B.C.	Cro-Magnon people, an early group of modern humans, inhabit Europe.
6000 B.C.	Agriculture develops and spreads through western Europe.
3000 B.C.	Civilizations develop on Crete and other Aegean islands.
800 B.C.	The Greeks start colonies throughout the Mediterranean region.
753 B.C.	Rome is founded on the Tiber River.
27 B.C. – A.D. 180	The civilization of Rome reaches its high point.
400s	The Middle Ages begin.
1300s	The Renaissance, a period of great progress in arts and learning, begins in Italy. It spreads through Europe during the next two centuries.
1347–1352	A plague, known as the Black Death, sweeps through Europe and kills about one fourth of its people.
1440	German goldsmith Johannes Gutenberg invents movable type. The ability to print copies of books more quickly contributes greatly to the spread of new ideas.
1689	The British government passes a Bill of Rights.
1700s	The Industrial Revolution begins, forever changing the cultural landscape of the continent.
1789	The French Revolution begins. At its conclusion in 1799, France is no longer ruled by a monarch.
1914 – 1918	World War I is fought throughout Europe.
1917	A communist dictatorship is established in Russia.
1939 – 1945	World War II is fought, largely on European soil.
1991	The Soviet Union dissolves as most of its republics declare their independence.
1993	The European Union is established.
2002	The euro replaces the traditional currency of many European countries.

How to Learn More about Europe

At the Library

Fischel, Emma. *Northern Europe.* Broomall, Penn.: Mason Crest Publishers, 2002.

Foley, Ronan. *The Rhine.* Austin, Tex.: Raintree Steck-Vaughn, 2003.

Foster, Leila Merrell. *Europe.* Chicago: Heinemann Library, 2001.

McNab, Chris. *Eastern Europe.* Broomall, Penn.: Mason Crest Publishers, 2002.

Porter, Malcolm. *Europe.* Austin, Tex.: Raintree Steck-Vaughn, 2002.

On the Web

Visit our home page for lots of links about Europe:

http://www.childsworld.com/links.html

Note to Parents, Teachers, and Librarians: We routinely verify our Web links to make sure they're safe, active sites—so encourage your readers to check them out!

Places to Visit or Contact

THE FIELD MUSEUM

*To see the "Moving Earth" exhibit and learn more
about the plates that form Earth's crust*

1400 South Lake Shore Drive

Chicago, IL 60605

312/922-9410

EUROPEAN UNION

To write for more information about Europe and the European Union

Delegation of the European Commission to the United States

2300 M Street, N.W.

Washington, DC 20037

202/862-9500

Index

About the Author

Cynthia Klingel has worked as a high school English teacher and an elementary school teacher. She is currently the curriculum director for a Minnesota school district. Cynthia Klingel lives with her family in Mankato, Minnesota.